CONQUER YOUR FEARS AND WIN

CONQUER YOUR FEARS AND WIN

GLORIA PATTERSON

Copyright © 2020 J Merrill Publishing, Inc.

All rights reserved. No part of this publication may be reproduced, distributed, or transmitted in any form or by any means, including photocopying, recording, or other electronic or mechanical methods, without the prior written permission of the publisher, except in the case of brief quotations embodied in critical reviews and certain other noncommercial uses permitted by copyright law. For permission requests, write to the publisher, addressed "Attention: Permissions Coordinator," at the address below.

ISBN: 978-1-950719-36-5 (Hardback)

ISBN: 978-1-950719-46-4 (Paperback)

ISBN: 978-1-950719-37-2 (eBook)

Library of Congress Control Number: 2020908592

Any references to historical events, real people, or real places are used fictitiously. Names, characters, and places are products of the author's imagination.

FRIST printing edition 2020.

J Merrill Publishing, Inc.

434 Hillpine Drive

Columbus, OH 43207

www.JMerrillPublishingInc.com

I will like to dedicate this book to God, who is the Head of my life, and the one who makes all things possible. My walk with God has made me the woman I am today, from brokenness to fullness. He is truly the leading and guiding force of my dreams. Without him, nothing is possible, with him all things are possible. My husband, Isaiah Hezekiah Patterson, for always encouraging and supporting me in all my endeavors and prays for me daily. My husband inspires me to do my best and tells me to leave the rest to God. My daughters, who I love and appreciate, Elisabeth, Hannah, and Naomi Patterson. My one stepdaughter Sarah Patterson, and to all my encouraging and powerful prayer warrior friends, church family, and family. I would like to thank my coach and mentor, Lashonda D. Gary. She inspires me through her teaching and Dream Build Success conferences, to keep pushing and believing in myself. Many inspiring friends, My Mary Kay Sales Director Lisa Snow, National Sales Director Yvonne Lemmon, friends, Brandy Horton, Audrey Peoples, Enola Franklin, Teressa Garcia, who are like my sisters and true family. My besties Irvette Dove (aka Toya) and Tyronica James, who's supported me from day one on this journey to success, and also my current book club friends Successful Women Rise. To God, be the glory to all my inspiring leaders who walked with me in this journey. I could not have done this without you all believing in me.

Without my leaders and friends standing in the gap for me, this could not have been possible. A special thanks to my mother n law Patricia

Patterson, who prays with me and helps me to stay focus on the important things of life. Co-worker Helena Boyd, who keeps me focused at work and treating me to fabulous lunches, and have a listening ear when I need her. To Janet Stephens, who helped me discover my publisher, Jackie Smith, Jr., and also the encourager and motivational speaker that enhances my life. "Those who seek the Lord lack no good thing." Psalm 34:10

CONTENTS

Introduction   ix

1. Overcoming Adversities   1
2. Procrastination   11
3. Desire   15
4. Affirmations   23
5. Children are a blessing   27
6. Hurricane Harvey   31
7. Love Your Spouse   41
8. Losing a Friend   49

About the Author   57

INTRODUCTION

"You can do all things through Christ that strengthens you," Philippians 4:13.

I spent the majority of my early childhood being told I wasn't good enough, smart enough, or worth loving. You don't realize how much of those negative words seep into your soul until you are faced with challenges.

I want you to join me on this journey through, "Conquer your fears and win," as I share with you how God helped me learn how to activate the winner in me. Too many of us have agreed with the negative words and losing spirit that keeps us in bondage. Today, it's time to break that losing streak and win. In each chapter, I will share my journey and the lessons I learned to help me have a winner attitude. Come on, are you ready to win?

This book is to inspire and encourage any woman who feels like they are not good enough. Also, if you have felt discouraged because of your upbringing, one of your parents left you, or whatever your circumstances were, it doesn't have to be your story. If you want to Win and overcome adversities, don't stop reading this book.

Introduction

This book is going to help you to arrive to new levels of thinking, growth, spiritual maturity. It will encourage you to change your mindset and let go and let God! And, enabling a winning mentality, not a loser mentality. Greatness begins with your thoughts. Believe that this is your season, and you were designed for greater, bigger, and better things.

If you have purchased this book, I want and need you to win! Winners win, and losers lose! Repeat this: I was wired to win, and I know losers are weak-minded. My breakthrough and change of mindset starts today!

The enemy, Satan, the devil, wants to keep you stuck in a rut and a bad mindset because with a bad mindset, you can't win. He comes to steal, kill, and destroy you because he hates that you are a child of God. So, why stay defeated? When Jesus died on that cross, He had you and me in mind so that you can have eternal life. Not earthly life, but eternal life. Make a change today, Win. Start today, and decide to be great.

Wake that sleeping giant inside of you and take back everything the enemy has stolen from you. Remember, you got this, and it's time to Win! Count your blessings and count your wins.

Has anyone ever told you that you are never going to be anything or that you are not good enough? Well, I was that girl. I was a girl who was told that you are not good enough, called stupid, dumb, and heifer. I mean, just verbally abused and tolerated, not loved by many.

I was bullied throughout middle school. What a life for a child, in an identity crisis, not knowing who I was as a child coming from a broken home, not raised by a father and mother. Desperate for love and looking in all the wrong places. My father and mother loved drugs more than they loved me. They were young-minded, dumb, confused, and in their teens. And, they didn't realize that they gave birth to something great, unique, and anointed. Has anyone experienced such?

Introduction

I can honestly say that I don't love them any less. The love I have for my parents is the same love God has for us, agape love. This kind of love comes from God, knowing him and having a relationship with his son, Jesus Christ. My parents were never married nor finished their education, but that didn't stop me. I was that misunderstood child with no identity, judged from birth. I didn't stand a chance to make it or become successful based on worldly expectations. But that's not what God

said the outcome was going to be.

When a child is separated from their parents at birth or an early age, it has what's called adverse childhood experience which is characterized as a stressful or traumatic event in a child's life that can lead to long term issues. When a child is physically separated from their parents, they can begin to experience what is known as toxic stress; that can have damaging effects on learning, behavior, and health across their lifespan.

Well, I came to tell you today, I was bought by the bloodstained banner, and that's called the blood of Jesus. Count your blessings and count your wins.

The hardest part of my life growing up without parents was the lack of support from them. Having parents to read the word of God to you at night, taking you to games, shopping, praying over you, or to just talk to when you are having those teen issues is important.

I had a lot of memory loss issues growing up, as well. It was just hard for me to retain information. I felt so insecure in my learning abilities and just in life period. It was a battle.

Parents don't understand the significance of birthing a child and, actually, raising your child.

Children need that love, so their brain can develop properly. I was grateful to have a praying great grandfather, but it's not the same. But

Introduction

I'm grateful that I had the Lord Jesus Christ by my side because if it weren't for praying grandparents, I would have been destroyed. Thank you, Jesus, for caring so much about me.

I pray for the mind of Christ, because of my memory and retention is so bad. Despite that, I was blessed to finish high school and college, even though my parents didn't, which made me the first generation to finish school. I now have a college degree as I graduated from Prairie View A & M University. I was blessed to finish high school and college, because my parents didn't, so that made me the first generation to finish school.

They also didn't maintain a corporate job either, never was employed with a career that lasted. My mother was going to be a nurse. Unfortunately, she didn't finish high school because she became pregnant with me at the age of 16, and my father was 18. He worked a little while in the field of construction after I was born. His father made him get a job because he had to take care of me. He didn't work longer than five years, because he chose a bad lifestyle - drugs and alcohol.

My mother developed a mental illness because of the hard drugs that they did together. Fortunately, it was after I was born, and not while my mother was pregnant, or I would have been a crack head baby. As I mentioned, it was a shame because they didn't realize that they gave birth to something special and great.

I do communicate with them both and love them with all my heart and soul. I don't hate them as my parents, but what I hated was the sin. Just like Jesus hates sin. I am so grateful that I survived those traumatic hardships. I was blessed to be taken in by my loving great-grandparents.

I was born in Robbins, Illinois, but raised in Wiggins, MS. I later attended college in Prairie View, TX. After college, I relocated to Houston, TX, and got married. After ten years of marriage and children, we settled in Katy, TX, before making the journey to Bexley, OH, after the devastation of Hurricane Harvey.

Introduction

As you will learn in further chapters, Hurricane Harvey took everything I had, including memories of material things I had for many years of my life. When you lose things, you realize that Jesus is the reason. That it's not just the things you need in life. It's the Lord Jesus Christ you need.

After the Hurricane, God was so good to me and my family that I never felt at a loss. I actually felt like I had won, that the best was yet to come and that the situation and devastation was just another chapter of my life.

Lessons in life are hard to understand, but challenges come to grow your faith and draw your heart closer to God. The enemy will always fight for your soul. But you can always stay ahead of him when you persevere in prayer and trust the Lord at his word.

I'm not ashamed to talk about the goodness of the Lord, because I know he is real, and will fight your battles if you allow him to.

As you continue to read this book, you will understand how I overcame weaknesses and had to trust God with all my faults and problems. I learned to take everything to God in prayer.

My prayer is that this book will inspire you to take bigger leaps of faith and win. You can conquer anything you put your mind to.

CHAPTER 1
OVERCOMING ADVERSITIES

I will never forget the memory of being dropped off and looking out of my great grandparents' screen door window, crying my eyeballs out. I felt as if my life was crashing, and I wasn't ever going to wake up.

Yes, at the age of five, you have a soul, and a deep scar of change, especially of course, when you don't get to choose your situation or outcome. Can you imagine being five years old and having to be dropped off with two people you didn't know, other than your birth parents?

I was confused and disturbed. I felt like my parents had abandoned me. They gave me up to strangers, not understanding as a five-year-old, this is my family, but what I knew at the time is that I didn't know them. At five, of course, I didn't understand a lot, but I knew my parents were leaving me.

My father had a drug and alcohol addition, but he still loved and cared for me. I didn't hate him, I hated the sin. My dad made a good decision to drop me off with my grandparents, and that's how I became the woman I am today. My mother didn't have a stable living environment, and developed a mental illness after the use of drugs. She was pregnant at 16, and her mother put her out at 18, she had to learn to survive in the streets. How sad was that?

My father was not ready to raise a child. He had the common sense to understand that after his mother passed with liver cancer, that he wasn't going to have the support to raise me, his daughter. He had all brothers, no sisters, so there were not going to be a stable woman to take the role of a parent.

He called his grandmother in Wiggins, MS, which was his mothers' mother to take the responsibility of raising me, and she, of course, said yes! My grandmother, my father's mom, passed when I was three years old. My life changed for the good once I left Chicago, IL. The devil thought he had me defeated at five years old, but he didn't. I knew deep down in my heart, and I would become very successful one day.

I remember the day I was dropped off with those strangers, my now deceased great grandparents Hugh Vanderbilt Sr. and Juanita Vanderbilt.

They were in their 70's when they took me in from two young parents who did not want the responsibility of a child because they were indulged in their lifestyle and habits. My parents were never married, my father had drug habits, and my mother had a mental illness due to drug abuse.

I was blessed to have two loving grandparents that took me in and raised me to become the woman I am today. I was raised in the church, New Welcome Hill Baptist Church, where Rev. Timothy Monroe was my pastor.

Wiggins, MS, was a small southern town with a population of 17,000 people. I attended head start through high school there. I grew up very sheltered and didn't have much brightness mentally. I was quiet, shy, and seeking love and attention from anyone who gave it to me.

My grandparents were very strict and ole school. They were all about church, school, cleaning the house, and getting your homework done, or you suffered. I didn't talk much because I was miserable, went to school, and got bullied all the time. So, I had a very tough upbringing.

I was a small-town girl with a big dream, big desires, and big ambitions. I was destined for greatness.

My parents had little education, but at least they made it to high school. My mother made it to the 11th grade and dropped out because of me, and my dad had to quit to work to help take care of me. He was a successful basketball player, could have made it to the pros. They did the best they could do, but God had a different plan for my life.

I share all of this because many people are suffering from an Identity crisis. They have been told lies about who they are, or better yet, they have believed a lie because of the verbal abuse, or suffered from anxiety because of coming from broken homes.

Mothers raising children alone, or like me raised by grandparents, have suffered from trauma in their childhood or going through trauma right now.

If you are reading this book, you may be struggling with who you are. The point is when God has a plan for your life, no matter what the devil tries to do, he will not Win! Do not stop dreaming, writing your visions, don't lose your identity based on where you come from or what you are going through.

You can do whatever you put your mind too. Don't allow no one or nothing to dull your sparkle. I was bullied as a little small-town girl, growing up with old people, kids would pick on me at school and say things like, "that's why your parents didn't want you, long-legged giraffe, and just ugly things. I was bullied from elementary school through middle school, and nothing stopped me. I had praying great grandparents, and that's what I knew. They loved me and prayed for me daily. They get the credit of who I am today.

The late Hugh Vanderbilt Sr. was a caring man of God, who loved the Lord, taught Sunday school, was the first man in church every Sunday morning, and the last one to leave every Sunday evening. I don't remember him ever missing a beat. And he made sure I didn't either.

This man was amazing and was the true hero in my life. He was always there for me. He made sure that I had all my needs met, that I was in church every Sunday, and at school being the best that I could be every day. He would always tell me, make sure you get your lesson and study.

He provided a roof over my head, clothes on my back, and hot meals every day. I didn't want for anything.

He was a man of greatness, and he wore many hats – he mowed yards, was the local loan shark, Sunday school teacher, and a parent raising a rebellious grandchild, yes me. I was proud to call him my grandpa, my hero.

The best day of my life is when he saw me walk across that stage at Prairie View A & M University to receive my bachelor's degree in Marketing. He was about 78 years old. I was so happy and proud to see the expression on his face that His prayers had been answered.

What an amazing accomplishment for me. My life was shattered at age 5, as I assumed, but it became a blessing and a real honor to know that God had his hands on my life and that the favor of the Lord was upon me. What a true celebration that day was.

On September 17, 2007, my day shattered again. My great grandfather, my hero, my biggest supporter and encourager, died from impact in a car accident, the worst day of my life.

He was healthy and strong and could have possibly lived another 10 to 20 years. Never was sick a day in his life, never hospitalized, or anything. A healthy man full of life and didn't even look his age.

He loved to ride his lawnmower to cut his grass on the weekends, sit in his favorite recliner chair, watch his westerns on Saturday morning, and his soap opera's every day of the week, I mean from the time they started at 11 am and ended at 3 pm!

He would wake up at the same time every morning, fall on his knees to pray, make his 1 cup of coffee, and eat his honey nut cheerios every single morning. I never saw him do anything different on any given morning.

He would also eat a mid-morning breakfast at 11 am or 12, like grits, toast, bacon, or sausage, but in the early mornings, he had a routine, and that's what I saw. He would rise before everyone to get things done.

I so appreciated him as my role model. God knew who to put in my life to make me strong, and a strong Black Woman at that. He was a true gift from God, a real man, and a provider. I never wanted or lacked for anything. What a Man!

When my great grandfather passed, I was married and had a 2-year-old daughter. So, my family had started to grow. I had the support system I needed in place to get over such a tragic accident.

My great grandmother passed when I was 11 years old. Comparatively, I didn't have as much of a relationship with her as I remembered with my great grandfather. But, I know that she loved me and wanted the best for my life.

She liked to travel and shop. I do remember that much about her because that's what I enjoy doing! She was very strict and firm, the kind of parenting we need for our youth today.

What she said goes. No, if's, and's, or but's about it, and no why's or talking back! You would find yourself picking up your teeth off the floor.

Grandparents back in my time were strong. They said what was on their mind and told it like it was. They were set in their ways and would get a belt whenever they needed to. I got the kind of spankings from my grandma that you had to pull your bottoms down, and she would lay you across your lap. I loved my grandparents; they were the rock of the family.

My paternal grandmother, whose name was Gloria Vanderbilt, was a trooper. I was the daughter she never had, but she took me in the first four years of my life. My grandmother and grandfather raised three biological sons and adopted two sons, so a total of five boys. Can you imagine such?

She was an amazing woman. I only got to hear a lot of stories about her, because I was so young. Her last words to her parents, Mr. Hugh and Mrs. Juanita Vanderbilt, before she died of liver cancer, to her parents Mr. Hugh and Mrs. Juanita Vanderbilt was were, will you raise my granddaughter? And the answer was yes. It was my great grandmother'sdecision and words because, at the time, my great grandfather's response was no, we are too old.

But see how God works. He had to take the liberty of raising me after she passed away when I was 11 years old, can you imagine such, a 70-year-old man having to take the responsibility of raising me, when he didn't even want me in the beginning. But at that moment he became my hero!

Truthfully, I never had a relationship with him until I was 12 years old. He was forced to take responsibility because he wanted to honor his daughter's wish and finish what my grandmother started.

He didn't know me, my likes, or my wants, because he never, at the time, got a chance to know me. It took the passing of my grandma for him to step it up. I hung around my great-grandma Juanita and only saw my grandpa, early in the morning or late in the evenings. He was always busy and felt that my grandma had everything taken care of with me, my wants, and my needs.

It was the hands of God that turned his heart, after her passing, and I genuinely believe that with all my heart. He was a very loyal, caring, and responsible man; he just didn't have time for me. Like I said earlier, he became my hero.

We talked every night on the side of his bed, he will always say just what I needed the most, made sure I was well dressed for school when he never cared at first. He took me to all my band practices. I played trombone in school. And he taught me how to drive a car.

The day I had to leave to go to college, Prairie View A & M University, he cried, that was the first time I ever have seen him cry. I didn't even see him shed a tear for my grandma's funeral, his wife unless he did it behind closed doors and didn't want everyone to know.

But the day I left was a sad day for him and me because we had bonded so well. All I could imagine what he felt in his heart was that his baby girl that he raised to be a Woman was all grown up, and that was his graduation day, and I salute him because I was a hard-headed, stubborn, rebellious child. After all, I was broken as a little girl, being dropped off with no identity of who was indeed my parents, and who was it that had their best interest in me. Confused, bitter, upset, in rage and scared, I was that girl.

When I got old enough to date, I was in unhealthy relationship after relationship, abusive relationships, and that was just dating guys. I was very promiscuous in my college years, looking for love in all the wrong places.

It took God to pull me out of the shadows of death. It took a praying great grandfather on his knees every single night and morning, a true impactful man of God whose heart is sold out for Jesus.

I am thankful for the experiences of life at that time because it made me stronger and helped me to become the Woman of God I am today, married to a powerful man of God, and blessed with three amazing children, which I will share more about in the next chapters. What the devil meant for harm, God turned it into good. Who would have thought a girl like me would have such a love for people. God is good!

I also had an Aunt, Delores P Vanderbilt, who stepped in to help my grandpa raised me, and he was her Father. She wasn't the nicest person, and we didn't get alone quite as much, because she verbally abused and did not really take the time to know me. She judged me from birth because of the mistakes my parents made. How do you just predetermine the outcome of someone's life without getting to know them first? That's the energy I felt from her. She was bitter, confused, troubled, and always mad. When she went to church, she would be happy to sing in the choir, but when she got home, she would make a quick rushed meal and go to her room and not engage in conversation other than gossip about the church folks on Sunday. That lady confused me so much.

I never knew what I was doing wrong to make her so angry. She made me do chores, would yell at me if I didn't want to or feel like it. She felt as if I was disrespecting her, but I eventually got on a routine, and that was something that helped me in life, which was structure.

She was the kind of person that was strict, firm, and set in her ways. What she said goes, and there were no ifs, ands, or, buts about it. I did learn how to be tough from her, strong, and independent.

I'm not going to say my life was hell because of her, but I was not always happy because of the way she dealt with me. I felt that it wasn't from Love, or because she wanted to do it. It was because she was forced to do it.

When my great grandmother passed, she told my grandpa that she would come down and help him raise me. But what I found out it was the perfect opportunity for her to come and be saved from financial woes, because she was in a lot of debt and distress.

When someone comes into your life because they must parent you, they are supposed to love you as their own, and she did not do that. Parenting or child rearing is the process of promoting and supporting the physical, emotional, social, and intellectual development of a child from infancy to adulthood. She was another authoritative figure in our home, but she did not parent me. It was more scolding than parenting. I was mistreated, verbally abused, physically abused, and neglected by her. It could have destroyed me.

It did for some of my school years and relationships with guys, but God gave me the strength I needed to overcome the weaknesses and the strength I needed to persevere through it. Therefore I give my grandfather credit for raising me and not her. Because He gave and showed me love, strength, confidence, took the time to sit down and have long talks with me, prayed with me and for me, and made many sacrifices for me.

My aunt changed by the time I reached my Junior and Senior years in high school and began to show me more support and help me with life. She was in my life from 7th grade to my senior year of High school. I forgave her for the way she treated me and our relationship, but it was some tough years to endure with her, very tough.

We should not settle for just being content, being ordinary, expand your thinking. There were days I was very complacent, confused, lost, and frustrated. My joy did not come until my faith increased, and a desire to fall in Love with Jesus, my personal savior, the man who died, and sacrificed his life for me. We all came to this world necked, wounded, and lost. The way you figure out who you are is by seeking a true, divine relationship with God. That is also the only way you will find out your purpose in life, and your dreams and desires will come clearer to you. Sacrifice time to spend quality time with your savior. He Loves you.

When you arise in the morning, seek him wholeheartedly, praise and worship him, thank him for being alive and well another day-Jesus Christ, the almighty, powerful, son of God.

My favorite song growing up was, "What a friend we have in Jesus." Hardships, suffering, confusion, lack of physical love, made my relationship stronger with God because in those times of struggling with my identity, and hardships, I didn't realize who I truly was in Christ.

It's through seeking scripture and desiring a closer relationship with Jesus Christ is what inspires you to keep going in life, or you will give up, result in medications, drugs, or whatever bad habits that lure your mind. The word of God says in Romans 12:2, "Do not be conformed to this world, but be ye transformed by the renewal of your mind, that by testing you may discern what is the will of God, what is good and acceptable and perfect."

We have to plead the blood of Jesus over our minds daily through prayer, so we won't fulfill the lust and desires of the flesh or be tempted by Satan. I found Christ two years after I graduated from college. I grew up in the church all my life, but that's not all you have to do. I was still lost, broken, scared, and confused until I sought a more purposeful relationship with God. The way you do that is by surrendering your will to Him and allow his Spirit to work through you.

You have to be willing to give up things of this world if you want a more purposeful relationship with God. He wants all of us, not just a 3rd, or half but all.

It took years for me to grow. It doesn't matter your age, all that matters is that you decide and just surrender. God will take you just as you are, wounded and scared. God knows that the Spirit is willing, but the flesh is weak. Pray this prayer for change:

"Lord, as I come to you in the name of Jesus, I surrender my will unto you.
I am tired, weak, and desire a closer relationship with you.
I have been angry, upset, lost, and confused.
Lord, help me to desire a closer walk with you and a purposeful relationship.
Lord, I'm tired of doing things on my own strength, search my heart take anything out of my heart that is not right, in Jesus' name I pray, Amen.

Sometimes we feel that we need to say a whole lot of words to get our point across, but God knows our hearts and everything about us. We just need to ask Him. I pray this helps.

May God bless you and strengthen you in Jesus' name, amen.

CHAPTER 2
PROCRASTINATION

James 1:8, "A double minded man is unstable in all his ways and cannot expect to receive nothing from God." So, when we pray, we must believe that we have received what we ask God for.

Do you procrastinate? I was a huge procrastinator. Procrastination is the avoidance of doing a task that needs to be accomplished. Procrastination is something you have to pray against if you have this weakness. It's almost like a slow dream killer. I procrastinated over ten years to work my business full time. I could have been a multi-millionaire by now. I wouldn't open my mail right away when it came, because I didn't want to face responsibilities.

We, as people, have been struggling with delaying, avoiding, and procrastinating on issues that matter to us. Procrastination can keep you from the right job, the right relationship, and can keep you in a bad mindset. When you understand procrastination and the science behind it, prayerfully, you will stop and began to improve your quality of life.

We create more work when we avoid what we are supposed to do. How ridiculous is that, right? This is also called a lack of self-control.

Procrastination is the act of delaying or postponing a task or set of functions. It prevents you from following through on what you set out to do.

If you are a procrastinator, all it means is that you like to avoid things that need to be done right now, in the present, because you haven't sent your brain a message that it's a sense of urgency.

Behavioral psychologists explain this as your present self and your future self. For example, when you set goals for yourself, like losing weight or writing a book or learning a language, you are making plans for your future self. You are envisioning what you want your life to look like in the future. They found that when you think about your future self, it is natural for your brain to see the value in taking actions with long term benefits. The Future self values long-term rewards, and the bottom line is, we want immediate gratification. When we don't get it, then we procrastinate.

For years I did not like myself. I was insecure, selfish, and stubborn. Procrastination was my way of living. It had become a comfortable lifestyle for me. I was satisfied with avoiding the truth, handling responsibilities; it was like an illness. If they had medication for procrastination, I would have been first in line.

The present self and future self are often at odds with one another. The future self wants to trim and fit, and the present self wants a doughnut.

Think about how the present self wants to save for the future. We know that we should, but the benefit of doing so is decades off, so it's far easier for the present self to see the value in buying a new pair of shoes than saving a $100 a month into a savings account, so 30 years from now you can retire and enjoy life.

Our brain values immediate rewards more highly than long-term rewards. Therefore, you might go to bed feeling motivated to make a change in your life. But, when you wake up, you find yourself falling back into old patterns. Your brain values long-term benefits when they are in the future (tomorrow), but it values immediate gratification when it comes to the present moment today. We must hold ourselves accountable for every choice we make.

The way I learned to do away with procrastination, I began to pray about it, because it was my biggest weakness and challenge in life. It's a spirit. I prayed and rebuked the spirit of procrastination.

I began to speak affirmations out loud like: I can do all things through Christ that strengthens me, I am smart, I am successful, I am great, I am loved, I am awesome. I was training my mind to be brilliant. The more positive words I spoke to myself out loud, the more my brain would take charge and act in the now.

Did you know the brain can heal itself, according to Dr. Caroline Leaf, we can control our thinking, our brain, with a 21-day brain detox? We control matter through our thinking and choosing. Thought leads to change in the brain. If you desire to do a 21-day brain detox, I highly recommend her book, author: Dr. Caroline Leaf.

Ask God to heal your mind of infirmities, which is a physical and mental illness. When we finally move beyond procrastination and act, you will be happier, feel less exhaustion, decrease the guilt of not taking care of business, and we won't feel discouraged or inadequate.

It's painful when we procrastinate, causes anxiety and stress. Who wants to live their entire life like that? Identify habits that make you procrastinate. Write it down, speak against it, and take action to change the story.

- Only listen to audiobooks or podcasts you love by exercising
- Only watch your favorite show while ignoring or doing household chores
- Only get a pedicure while processing overdue work emails or any
- Only eat at a favorite restaurant when you have accomplished a successful week of "No Procrastinating."

Reward yourself when you feel as if you have achieved a big task and didn't procrastinate. The bottom line stops procrastinating because its dead weight its an illness, that only God can heal.

Pray a prayer over yourself every night before you go to bed, and ask God to:

- heal your mind,
- help you to stop procrastinating,
- heal you from any infirmities of the brain
- heal you from insecurities

That could be a stronghold because of what your parents did when you were inside of their wound. A lot of problems that occur in our lives are because of our parents' choices and mistakes they made, and we are a seed of that, and we must pray against that stronghold and ask God to forgive them for what they have done. Plead the blood of Jesus every day and night over your mind.

God will heal you. I can truly say He has healed me, and I'm grateful. I would not be the woman I am today if it wasn't for the blood of Jesus. Praying earnestly that He will forgive my parents for what they did, so I could be set free.

Those who are set free are free indeed. God is not a man that should lie. Our heavenly Father is waiting for us to come to him in prayer.

Be bold about what you want from Him and stand strong. Don't be double-minded. The word of God says in James 1:8, "A double minded man is unstable in all his ways and cannot expect to receive nothing from God."

So, when we pray, we must believe that we have received what we ask God for. He also says in James 1:5, "If any of you lack wisdom, let him ask of God, that giveth to all men liberally, and upbraided not; and it shall be given him. But let him ask in faith, not wavering."

CHAPTER 3
DESIRE

Desire Jesus more in your life daily. Without him, and desiring more of him, I would have just been a small-town girl, with no desires, or ambitions. I was a "just do what you told" type of girl, go to school, get your education, and get a job.

I would tell anyone you should always desire more than just existing, just live to die; that's what I call it.

Without Jesus dying on that cross, we wouldn't even exist. So why waste your time doing nothing, being a nobody?

Desire to be great because greatness is within.

The world has enough challenges, negativity, and deadweight. People just exist with no ambitions. The world needs more people to inspire others to become successful.

We all have a seed of greatness in us because of who created us. We were born from a seed of God. So, if we come from the creator of the heavens and the earth, then we all have greatness inside of us. Isn't that amazing?

Let go and let God, be authentic, pray and ask him to help you build a relationship with him, and die to self daily. Is it easy? No. Is it a sacrifice? Yes.

When you truly love someone, you must make their lives apart of your life. You must spend quality time with them to get to know them and to let them know you truly love them, and that's by spending time with them.

Take action. Ask God to draw your heart closer to him. Ask him to place you in the palms of his hands. Ask God to lead you, guide you, and strengthen you.

God is a rewarder of those who diligently seek him. According to Hebrews 11:6, "But without faith it is impossible to please God, those who come to God must believe that He is, and that He is a rewarder of those who diligently seek Him." We must have Faith, trust him, acknowledge him in all that we do; it is He that directs our path.

We become negative and discouraged by the way we think. You can be controlled by others, or you can make a decision, and decide that you are going to be great.

I like that scripture that says, "Those who wait upon the Lord shall gain new strength they shall mount up with wings like eagles, they shall run and not grow weary and walk and not grow faint," Isaiah 40:31.

We deceive ourselves when we say I can't do this, or I can't do that. "You can do all things through Christ that strengthens you," Philippians 4:13. That's the lie the enemy wants us to believe, "I can't."

He wants you to stay stuck in a mindset that will not allow you to be free. Please know that Jesus loves you, and He wants the best for your lives. The enemy is a defeated foe in the name of Jesus! And the blood of Jesus Christ is against Satan and all his Demons. Believe growth, power, endurance, and your morals will begin to expand.

Be a victor, not a victim of your circumstance. Jesus came and died on that cross, so he could set us free, and liberate us from bondage, captivity.

On this journey of success, I had a mentor and coach, Lashonda D. Gary. She is a powerful, phenomenal speaker and encourager, inspire women to be great, success-minded, and she leads people to Christ. She is also authentic and genuine, truly passionate about the Lord and her walk with Him. She encourages you and I to do the same.

When you grow up with negative people, you need the strategy of finding mentors, people that can encourage you, and inspire you. It's great to have a mentor, a coach, someone with wisdom to encourage you. Consider a group or organization that will build you, uplift your spirits, and inspire you.

On this growth journey and path, I decided to take in life. I was a part of Mary Kay cosmetics, a powerful organization of powerful leaders and mentors. I listened to a lot of motivational cd's, inspiring YouTube videos, and read several inspirational books. My favorite author was Joyce Myers. She is a powerful author and speaker.

Brokenness

I've been so broken and scared Living afraid and not serving the Lord God Almighty, and it comes from insecurity, doubt, fear, confused about who you are in Christ Jesus. It wasn't until the fall of 2017, when I became purposeful, losing a home and all my material possessions. If I didn't know the Lord, I would have been broken for good.

God gave me the strength to keep going and hold my head up higher than before.

I remembered the scripture that said, "No good thing will I withhold from those who walk uprightly," Psalms 84:11. He gives us promises in his word, the bible that He gives us the strength we need daily.

God is so merciful. He restores our strength and helps us get through suffering and pain.

My family went through hurricane Harvey in 2017, and I never wondered not one time why me. I knew in my heart that, if God allowed it to happen, then he was going to take care of me and bless me with more than I had. And, He did exactly that.

It became a season of blessings. FEMA wasn't alone in helping us. We received blessings from churches, church family, friends, and scarcely our family.

I can count on my fingers how many family members helped, and it was mind-blowing. I never really had a strong family support system, and that would bother me, that they rather see you struggle than rising. But when God's got you, you don't worry about that either. On that note, he gave me the scripture Psalms 23:

The Lord is my shepherd, I lack nothing. He makes me lie down in green pastures, he leads me beside quiet waters, he refreshes my soul. He guides me along the right paths for his name's sake. Even though I walk through the darkest valley, I will fear no evil, for you are with me; your rod and your staff, they comfort me. You prepare a table before me in the presence of my enemies. You anoint my head with oil; my cup overflows. Surely your goodness and love will follow me all the days of my life, and I will dwell in the house of the Lord forever."

My mentor and coach, Lashonda D. Gary, mentored me through Facebook ministry and her web classes. I began listening to her every day, and it gave me the momentum I needed to get my book started and begin writing.

I learned very well in my Mary Kay Journey to surround yourself with powerful, positive thinking people who were going somewhere in life and had dreams and aspirations in life.

I went through several seasons of brokenness. feeling discouraged, insecure, lifeless, even my marriage, and work began to drain me every day and suck the life out of me. There were times I could not get focused or had the energy to work my part-time Mary Kay business or read a positive book. I would just feel drained.

I experienced several seasons of brokenness, fear, tiredness, and feeling defeated. Probably a little depressed, but I didn't like speaking words like that because what you think about you bring about. So I couldn't and wouldn't self-sabotage myself like that.

The power of words grows and manifests itself, and I have read enough motivational, inspirational books to not think and believe like that. And not only that, I was a strong and powerful woman, child of God, child of the King.

I knew that the enemy wanted to stunt my growth too, he was a liar, and I knew I couldn't allow him to win.

We moved to a small town called Bedias, TX, in July of 2015. One of the worst experiences in my life. My drive to work was an hour and 30 minutes going to work and coming back. Waking up at 4:30 a.m. to leave the house at 5:30 a.m., with three tired children, as well. Having to prepare them and get them ready too. It was the most exhausting and draining experience ever in my life. We did that for six months.

Let me tell you how good God is, he allowed mold to grow inside the bathroom walls, and we were forced to move. I also had been praying for a miracle. I was tired of driving so much, and the wear and tear on my body, and my children wasn't worth it anymore.

My husband wanted the experience and knowledge of living in the country. I knew he wanted that opportunity to grow a garden, have chickens and animals. So, he sold me the idea, and I accepted it.

He was good at selling me a lot of ideas, and of course, when it's your husband, you just roll with the punches. This experience was good and bad. The good was it taught me to fight through the pain and remain steadfast, and the bad was too much to handle regarding my health. God protected us on those dark roads every single day. It would be dark when we leave in the morning and dark when we come home.

My children would sleep on the hour and a half drive, and dinner time, they would have already eaten in the car, or on the drive home before they fell asleep. God carried us, and I have no complaints now that he delivered us.

You learn through struggle and hardships that trouble won't last always. When you are a child of God, it comes to strengthen you and to grow your faith in the Lord Jesus Christ.

Another blessing that came out of the Bedias experience was our dog named Rex, and our cat named Juliet. We had to give our dog away when we moved because we couldn't take dogs to the next apartment home we lived in, because he was so big, and half rottweiler and pit-bull. He was the prettiest dog and so sweet. He was the first dog I ever owned, and I was so heartbroken when I gave it away.

Our cat had the privilege to go with us to the apartment, because my oldest daughter Elisabeth was very attached, and she would have been heartbroken and terrified. She loved her cat; it became her best friend.

I never could get attached to Juliet like I did our dog, Rex. But Hurricane Harvey decided to come and swept our home away. I went back after a week to save her, and I grew close to her.

Seeing that look in her eyes, the devastation that she had gone through tore me apart. the thought that she was possibly dead, and seeing my daughter Elisabeth cry about it, tore me apart.

So, I began to pray for the cat to be alive when we went back to check on our place and belongings. The reason we left her was that we never thought it was going to be that devastating. We assumed that we would go back after three days to our home.

When I got home to see the damage, our home was destroyed, it smelled like dead people, and the 4 feet of water inside our home left everything destroyed. I can't explain how awful that smell was, and our cat Juliet was still alive.

She experienced the whole hurricane storm. When I rescued her, her eyes were dilated. She had been so terrified.

It was one week later before we were able to drive back into Houston. Roads and highways had been blocked. There was no entering the city for a week. Streets were blocked off, and it was awful. God protected our cat through the storm because of my prayers. I truly believe that's how she became my best friend. I began to love on her and show her some affection.

We must desire more prayer in our lives. We must pray to God daily and ask to be delivered. We go through season after season, year after year not being delivered, because we are afraid to ask, seek, and knock. We must stop being afraid of prayer and allowing that whisper of demons to tell us prayer is not going to help us nor deliver us.

Don't pray only when you feel like it, that's called emotional prayers to God, and that is not honoring him. He deserves more respect from us than emotional prayers.

Don't pray when it's only convenient for you. The bible says to pray always, that's the tool we must use to fight the devil and his demons.

God is not a Genie in the sky. We must come boldly to the throne of grace. Pray to be delivered from doubt, fear, past and present sins, jealousy, and covetousness.

Most of the time, those are the things that are holding us back. It keeps us in bondage. We need to become all that God has called us to be. You are a child of the king. Don't forget that anytime you feel defeated, say to yourself, I'm a child of the king.

CHAPTER 4
AFFIRMATIONS

- I am fearfully and wonderfully made.
- I was designed and made perfect in the eyes of God.
- I am designed for greatness.
- I am unique.
- I am intelligent.
- I walk with authority.
- I am strong.
- I am powerful.
- I am creative.
- I am brilliant.
- I am blessed.
- Everything my hands touch is blessed.
- I am favored by the Lord and people.
- I was born to be successful, great, unique, different, and inspired.
- I am motivated to win, driven to lead others.

When you think abundantly and infinitely, you began to open and expand your thinking even more. You will start to see it, believe it, and create your dreams, future, and plans.

If you are the type of person I was, always looking for help and handouts, I would advise you to stop.

When you need a blessing from the Lord, you must be a giver. It's not easy, but you must begin to take your eyes off of self because you are blocking your blessings. You can start giving small, and it will impact your life. It will inspire you to move forward in the knowledge and wisdom of Love. Like the scripture says, "Do unto others, as you would have them to do to you, Luke 6:31." "Love your neighbor as yourself," Mark 12:30. There is no commandment greater than this.

When we do for others, it comes back to us. I have experienced this numerous times.

I can say that I was very selfish in my adult years. I wanted others to do for me and help me. That concept was wrong thinking, and I suffered many years thinking like that.

When you are always in a receiver and not a giver, is that glorifying God, or is that helping you? If you have a dream to be the best, to win, or grow, you must begin to pray and ask God what I can do to help someone today. How can I be a light, who can I bless today. Is there a charity I can give to or donate clothes, or a church, a booster club? Who needs food, clothing, water, a light bill paid, we all know these responsibilities come like clockwork.

When we begin to think of others, the blessings flow like a river. It can be someone in your family, your circle of influence, or a divorced woman with children. Sometimes we are waiting for a promotion from God, and He is simply waiting for us to move forward.

Take control of your life, act today, right now, don't wait another second. God loves a cheerful giver. If you have lost sight of who you are and your identity, then "Let go and Let God."

Pray that he will lead and guide you. God wants us to come to him. He says, "Come to me, all you who are burdened, and I will give you rest. Take my yoke upon you and learn from me, for I am gentle and humble in heart, and you will find rest for your souls. For my yoke is easy and my burden is light." Mathew 11:28-30.

Pray this Prayer:

Dear Lord, I surrender my will unto you. I am tired of doing things my way. I do not have the results my heart desires, so I need your help, today, Lord! I look up to you, Lord, right now in the Name of Jesus, forgive me of my wicked ways. You are God, and you are a rewarder of those who diligently seek you. You said early in the morning we shall seek your face. I would like you to transform in me a new heart, a new mind, and a new body. Thank you, Lord, in advance for answering my prayer in Jesus' Name I pray, Amen.

CHAPTER 5

CHILDREN ARE A BLESSING

When I became pregnant with my three daughters, Elisabeth, Hannah, and Naomi, who are very active, and an inspirational part of my life. I did not plan any of my births. I was financially distressed, bent out of shape, burdened with bills, debt, almost lost my car, just clueless of who I was. I knew I was Child of the King, Child of God, but I had no identity. I didn't understand my worth.

You heard my story at the beginning. My parents were very young; they birthed me out of wedlock; gave me up to grandparents that I didn't know. I was not confident that I could be a mother.

What would I do with a child? Could I possibly give them what I thought I never had, which was love, security, confidence, peace, happiness? All the things God gives, but I didn't know or understand that at the time.

God was truly the head of my life. The reason He blessed me with three girls and a husband is that He gave me what I never had, and that was a family. See, isn't God good? He loves us so much.

God is the only one that can give you identity, true love, confidence, and security. Man can't do those things, only God, because he is the reason we exist.

God matures you and gives you more and more wisdom by reading His Word. We, as a generation of people, must get to that place in our mind that God cures all things if we seek him. He says in his word, "Seek ye first the kingdom of righteousness, and all these things will be added unto you."

When you spend quality time with God, He will speak to you. You shall Desire to want more. My children are the reason my heart desires more; without them, I honestly believe I would have been deeply scarred and, in the World, of lost people and sinners. God did not want that for my life.

Our blessings are right in front of us, and we don't even know it. We need to wake up from sleep and slumber and look around and in front of us. Pay attention to your current blessings, everything around you. God has already given you a lot of what your heart desires and have been seeking.

Just continue to follow your dreams, write your goals, your vision, and continue to press forward. Don't let no one tell you, "you can't." You can do all things through Christ that strengthens you. Tell Satan to get thee behind you in the Name of Jesus, who shed his blood on Calvary for you so that you can be free.

My daughters Elisabeth and Hannah became entrepreneurs to inspire Women and children. Elisabeth, at her 11th bday party, received a bead set to make bracelets. She began to turn it into a hobby, something to do for fun.

She later decided to turn it into a business. She then decided to sell them for $3 at the Katy Mills Mall. She sold all of them in 30 min with only ten made bracelets on her arm. She and her sister Hannah were selling the bracelets for $3.

Conquer Your Fears and Win

They began doing so well, they raised their prices to $5 and $10, Hannah catered her bracelets to small children, and Elisabeth catered her bracelets to women. Elisabeth has always been crafty. She enjoyed drawing and loves to make things; she can take a box and build a Barbie dream house.

When they came up with the idea to sell bracelets, I thought it would be something cute and fun to inspire women and children. Then it turned into an inspirational business.

They named their business Embrace. They were confident about selling their bracelets because they got their inspiration from watching me talk to women about Mary Kay and inspiring them. Children are intelligent, and they model what their parents do. After Elisabeth began to do so well, she raised her price to $10 a bracelet, next it will be $15. I'm so proud of my daughter being a light to her sisters and the youth of today's world, deciding to become ambitious with absolutely no training, just planning to do something different and inspirational to encourage people. The words she came up with were:

- encourage, confident, brave,
- courageous, inspire, success,
- successful, believe, achieve,
- succeed, love, happy,
- joy, blessed, smile, trust, and grace.

Grace was their top-selling bracelet. Elisabeth is going to start her own college fund, car fund, and apartment fund. She was confident that she could do this, become very successful, and make it happen.

Children don't make excuses like we, adults, because they haven't learned doubt, fear, incompetence, and all the lies that we tell ourselves, to let us off the hook. We, as individuals, learn these mindsets, this is called learned behavior. These girls made between $100-$175 each, in an hour and 30 minutes, being in the mall. Just amazing. God is so good.

CHAPTER 6
HURRICANE HARVEY

August 27, 2017, Hurricane Harvey came-this was the time when my life changed and did a 180 degree turn around. It was the first of devastation I had ever experienced in my adult life. My family and I lost everything.

The day before the storm, we drove to Dallas, TX. I was at work on Thursday, hearing that a category 1 or 2 storm was developing in the gulf. Of course, your first thoughts are, "Oh, It's probably not going to be so bad." But, when your gut feeling tells you it will be bad, you listen.

Well, my husband and I decided at first to buy lots of water, stock up on perishables, and to gas up the cars in case we decided to leave. No one ever thinks it's going to be that bad because it never really is. But this was the worst of the worst ever in the state of Texas.

My heart was broken, a state of emergency like never. I had a dream years before that a flood took us out, and back then that was a sign from God, to be prepared for the worst.

My husband was never a worrier, but I am. And I don't see it as worrying; I perceive it as a concern or being cautious because this can be bad.

Well, later that evening, we were watching the news, and it changed from a Category 2 storm to a 3, or possibly 4. That's when we became sure, let's just go to Dallas to wait this storm out.

My husband was still like, are you sure? I don't think anyone is leaving, because I don't believe it's going to be that bad.

I heard God's voice clear, and He said to leave. And the way I knew is because I prayed to God, "if it's not meant to leave, don't give me any peace." And I didn't. No peace came to me whatsoever about staying. I'm so glad I listened to the voice of the Holy Spirit, we would have been leaving on a boat.

The stores were running out of water, perishables, and everything was running low in all stores. I heard all these things at work from social media.

I called my husband to ask him had he picked up water or food. He told me no, not yet. I had to ask him to stop procrastinating.

I had to go to Elisabeth's volleyball game that evening. So I was not able to do any of the shopping. I had no food in the house because I hadn't been grocery shopping. I was very concerned that we were not going to last on food with everything running out in the stores.

That's why, in times like these, you must remain faithful and close to God, because you are not going to have the strength to make it without him. That oil of doing things your way will run out. I am the kind of person that shops when we need to, not for two or three weeks at a time, because in our home things would go bad, not last.

That evening began to look ugly. There was nowhere to find water, and gas stations were running out of gas. So I began to pray, Lord, where can we find water. He reminded me of a gas station in our neighborhood that had water and gas for our vehicles. That's what you call a relationship with God. He will lead and guide you exactly where to go when you spend time with him.

My husband wanted to go home and take a nap before we drove to Dallas. I woke him up at 4:30 am and told him lets go before the roads get crowded like it did when we went to Ft Worth, TX, for Hurricane Ike. That was predicted to be bad, as well.

Everyone was on the road for that scare. But with Hurricane IKE, nothing really happened. Just harsh rain, some flooding, power outages, and fallen trees. Some people's lights were out for a while, but that was about it.

When we decided to get on the road about 4:30 am, no one was hardly on the road, no traffic or anything. So my husband began to believe that we were wasting our time, but I still had the same gut feeling. I was so glad I followed my intuition and the Lord's voice because we came home to nothing.

It was hard losing our things, my family was distraught, but everything that we lost, God multiplied it. We had church family, friends, and very little family support.

Family?? We received way more support from strangers than family. But that's how God works. I knew deep down inside of my spirit that God had us in the palm of his hands. His promise says He will never leave us nor forsake us.

I knew from growing up with a praying grandfather that I was a Child of the King. I hadn't really lost anything, just material things. These things could be replaced.

When I say God showed up in our lives, right when we needed him too, he showed up. My family didn't lack anything. We gained more than we lost. The greatest blessing was we had each other, and we had our lives. You don't worry when you know who you serve. Therefore, it is so important to stay close to Jesus. I believe if I wasn't close to Jesus. I would have worried, suffered, and struggled.

Trust him, folks. He wants all your heart, not half, not a surface-based relationship. Meaning, don't serve him only when you want something or want to be blessed. But always even during a storm or a breakthrough. I realized that trouble only lasts a season. Trials come to test us, test our hearts, to see if we truly love the Lord like we say we do. Blessings come when we are ready to receive them, or when we have passed a test. God says, taste to see that the Lord is good, and blessed are all who trust upon him, Psalm 34:8.

Well back to storm Harvey, my husband calls and says I was only able to get a few things, and there was no water. So I prayed, and I was like Lord, where can I find more water, and a gas station in our neighborhood came to my mind. I also remembered we needed to gas up our vehicles. Every gas station you can think of was running out of gas. It was like we were living in the last days.

People were storing up, gassing up, and everyone was prepared to weigh the storm out. Hearing and listening to several people say it's not going to get that bad. The news always says that we are going to stay right here.

When my daughter and I returned home from her volleyball game, I did not feel right. The Spirit in me was warning me that it was going to be bad. I never felt that kind of way before. Kind of like when I first met my husband, the Spirit said, "He's the one. He is going to be your husband, and that was so.

I cried out to my husband that evening and said, "babe, we need to leave. I believe it's going to be bad."

He says, "You really think so,?" I'm like, yes!

My husband says, let me take a nap. Then, we will go to Dallas. Call up our friends Yvonne and David. I called and explained to them what was going on. They said, yes, come on down. We would love to have you all. So later that night, our daughter, Hannah, was watching YouTube on Television, and a married couple was speaking. She says mommy listen to this, they're talking about if there is a hurricane category 1, 2, 3 or whatever category it is, leave!

The news was not informing people to evacuate. But when I heard the message, it was confirmed that we should go.

We started the drive to Dallas on Friday evening, the weekend of the storm, at 4 am. We were the only ones on the road. I wanted to beat the masses, just in case. But my husband began to second guess our decision and thought that we were making a huge mistake leaving Katy.

Well, I knew in my heart, Spirit, and soul that we were making the right decision. We drove through the morning and arrived in Dallas at our friends' house at about 10 am.

Back at home, the severe raining and thunderstorms began at about 2 am Saturday and continued all day Saturday and Sunday night, August 27. The Hurricane became a full category 4, leaving flooding, heavy rains, and people losing their homes due to the floods.

Now we were watching this on the news. I couldn't take my eyes off the television. I was glued to the television screen all day Sunday and Monday.

I began to pray for everyone because it was looking terrible. In Dallas, it was beautiful, sunny with light rain. I was sad for others, but I was happy we decided to leave. I can honestly share that I had no peace for a week. I was concerned about being stuck in Dallas and not being able to return home.

I received a call on Tuesday, August 29, 2017, from a good friend, Mistee, that our apartment home was on the news underwater. I immediately cried and said, "No!" Tears were gushing down my face. No, why, Lord, why me!!!

The children ran into the room, where I was on the phone asking what's wrong? "I'm like our home is gone!" It flooded! My husband, children, and I were furious, as well. So while we were officially homeless with no home to go back to, we also couldn't enter back into the city of Houston. The roads and freeways were closed, so we had no clue when we would be able to return.

My friend worked at North Dallas Adventist Academy, a private Christian school in Dallas, TX. She called the principal and asked if my kids would be able to attend school because they were displaced and homeless. They agreed to allow them to attend school, and our children were thrilled.

They were excited to go to school there, and everyone treated them so kindly. The teachers and students were great, welcoming, helpful, and, most importantly, understanding. What would I have done without the grace of God?

Isaiah and I had 8 hours a day to plan and think about what we do next. First, we had to apply for Fema. I mean, can you imagine we lost everything. We only packed 3 to 4 outfits. My oldest daughter Elisabeth didn't pack anything. I knew without faith that I could not go on. What an excellent opportunity to exercise my faith.

We didn't have any money saved to get a new place, or a temporary home. We had to depend on friends and wait for financial assistance. Who plans for this kind of disaster? The rich, I'm sure.

Well, the new chapter of our lives began. We planned for a week. A week later, early Friday morning, September 3, 2017, we took the girls to school and drove to Houston. We took a risk.

We arrived in Houston at 11 am and saw all the damage and high waters. We had to take several back roads. It was horrible to see Houston was at its worst.

I was very saddened about the devastation. We took so many detours and didn't arrive at our place until 5 pm that evening. Traffic was bad, and cars were bumper to bumper. I thought we would never make it.

Well, when we made it to our side of town, it was clearly underwater. We had to take a boat to our home. When we arrived, the water had receded, but our place was gone. Our home smelled like sewer, dead animals, dead people, I mean ruined. I couldn't salvage anything. I had to count it all a loss.

Our cat that we carelessly left behind was still alive. We left her only to be gone for the weekend we believed, and we left her plenty of food and water. She was in her favorite place when we arrived; at Elisabeth's bed. I was so grateful she was still alive.

We prayed for her the entire time we were away. My daughter had been torn about her. We packed her up and brought her with us back to Dallas. The cat was in shock. We could tell she suffered a lot of anxiety. We pampered her back with love. Elisabeth was so happy when we arrived with her. She was her best friend.

The water only came about 4 ft high. But enough to damage our home. It was moldy, smelly, and not at all livable. We knew after losing everything. God had a plan for our lives.

The move to Ohio

We stayed in Dallas with friends for two full weeks, then stayed with a friend in Humble, TX for a week. She was a good friend that I've been knowing from the church. She had a huge home and welcomed all of us to stay for three days.

Three families offered us to stay if we needed too. So, my husband had me choose, and I decided to stay with the family who went above and beyond for us, they were so welcoming. They grocery shopped for us, cooked meals, and had a key made for my husband and me. No one does that, but God. It is God who moves on the heart of man, and I am so grateful for that.

We lived with them for three months. I continued to work at Katy ISD as a paraprofessional. Isaiah continued to do landscaping, and then we decided to move to Ohio.

I was not feeling Ohio. Everything inside of me was working against moving to Ohio. My Husband was very determined to move there, because his mother had an empty home that she hadn't lived in for eight years, and was still paying the rent on.

I was nervous to see what we were going to see once we arrived, but she did have a neighbor friend who would check on it from time to time. We stayed in a hotel for a week, once we arrived, and went back and forth to clean it and get it prepared. It wasn't so bad. God got us through it all.

We traveled through two states, Mississippi and Tennessee, and it wasn't so bad. I had my best friend in Mississippi and my Father in Tennessee. We had the opportunity to spend quality time with them.

Fema had blessed us. And churches had blessed us. We were okay, financially. Money was not an issue for us at all. We had more than enough. We had the support of strangers, as well. People knew what we had gone through, and they gave it to us. We didn't know them from Adam, but that is just how God works.

My children did not want for anything. They had to be out of school for two months. We had to get them adjusted to an unfamiliar environment, new friends, and people. It was tough for them, don't get me wrong. But they adjusted well after three months in school.

The school was known to be the top school system in OHIO, so that was a plus. We were living in Bexley, OH, the place where a lot of Jews lived. It is a lovely little suburb of Columbus, OH. I knew I could manage.

If my girls were happy and adjusting, I could adapt and be happy. The 3rd week of December, a week before Christmas, I got hired at a private school called Columbus Adventist Academy. I started as a substitute teacher and loved it. The staff was good to me, and I enjoyed working with the children as well.

Four months of being in Ohio, I started applying for more jobs and landed with a company, Mettler Toledo, three weeks later. It was like an answer to prayer.

I was so relieved to find a job that paid me well. It was a blessing. God knew what I needed, and it was right on time.

Life began to get better and better, and I continued to work my Mary Kay business, as well. I found an amazing sales director and started going to their Monday night success meetings. She was also an answer to prayer, and her name was Brittani. It was where 3 to 5 Sales directors met and trained us, consultants. I didn't have to pay to attend her meetings, it was in a church building, and I have been blessed from attending. Mary Kay is a true blessing to me. It keeps me focused and happy. I love the energy from the women in Mary Kay; they're always happy and energetic.

What a phenomenal company that inspires women and produce millionaires. I'm praying and believing for Directorship, and it will happen. I desire the right women on my team, prayer warriors, not just anybody, but people who believe in the Power of God and what He can do for them and their families.

God is real, and He is a rewarder of those who diligently seek Him. He will show me how to do it, with prayer and fasting. He can also show you how to make your dreams come true, just trust him, have faith, unwavering faith, believe, achieve, and conquer. Faith without works is dead. Follow through, stop procrastinating, and say affirmations daily.

God is powerful and mighty and able to do above and beyond what we can imagine. Please trust Him, get to know Him better if you don't. Sing songs of admiration. It will encourage you to seek Him with your whole heart. I can't do anything without God by my side. He is the reason we exist, and we need to follow Him. In Philippians 3: 7-10, scripture says, "But whatever gain I had, I counted as loss for the sake of Christ. Indeed, I count everything as loss because of the surpassing worth of knowing Christ Jesus my Lord. For His sake I have suffered the loss of all things and count them as rubbish, In order that I may gain Christ and be found in Him, not having a righteousness of my own that comes from the law, but that which comes through faith in Christ, the righteousness from God that depends on faith that I may know him and the power of his resurrection, and may share his sufferings, becoming like him in his death."

Knowing and Learning biblical scripture is the key to our success in following Christ. He is the way, the truth, and the light. There is no other way, so lean not to your own understanding but follow God in all your ways, and He will direct your path.

CHAPTER 7

LOVE YOUR SPOUSE

I am happily married to a man of God. A powerful prayer warrior who has been an answer to prayer, a true blessing and gift from God. My husband's full name is Isaiah Hezekiah Patterson, isn't that powerful? A biblical name, and I'm so grateful. I prayed for a man of God.

When I first met him, he prayed over a brain pituitary tumor. I had been on medication for a year before I met him. My situation was rare; a lot of people never heard of it. When I shared with him what I was going through, he said I am going to be praying over it. I told him, okay, yes, I'll be in agreement with you.

I went to the doctor three months later for a follow-up appointment. They didn't see anything. I was so happy that I had been healed, the power of prayer. God had answered our prayers, and I was so grateful.

I was the one who experienced and dated a lot of knuckleheads. You remember the story at the beginning; I was looking for love in all the wrong places because I wasn't born from love or a covenant of God. I married my husband, my knight in shining armor, on September 22, 2004.

This man lived in the apartment complex, where I resided. He was handsome, strong, and very confident in who he was. And most importantly, a prayer warrior, a man after God's own heart.

I had never felt the way he made me feel when we first met, love at first sight. He walked into the computer room of our complex, smiling from ear to ear as if he had just won a million dollars. I got a chill like never before when I looked into his white pearly eyes.

In my mind, I was like, who is this man, and why do I feel like this? Well, guess what? I had no idea this man was going to be my husband.

I was in denial at the time we met. I was preparing to end a relationship with a knucklehead. We exchanged phone numbers on that day in October 2003. I was working on something very important and needed to save some information on a floppy disk, and he happened to have one. Yes, back then it was a floppy disk, now just save to a flash drive, or email a copy to yourself.

After that day, I never called him. We met again six months later, which happened to be on his birthday, April 15, 2004.

He was riding his bike. I was working a job going business to business for AT&T and we spoke.

He says, don't I know you?

I looked and said, "no."

He says, "you're Gloria,"

I'm like, "yes, well, nice to see you again."

Then he says, "it's my birthday, and I decided to ride my bike."

I said, " okay, it's your birthday, and you are riding your bike."

I'm like, okay! Well, guess what? I was single at that point. I decided to leave that knucklehead, and honestly made a decision that I wasn't going to date for a while, because I had such bad taste for choosing good men.

I felt they didn't know how to treat me or make me feel special, loved, and appreciated. At this point in my life, I started praying for the right man and relationship. He had to be a Man of God and on fire for Christ.

Isaiah was that Man. The man I had prayed for and didn't know until our first date.

He invited me to a revelation seminar at his church. No man ever wanted to take me to church on a first date. As a matter of fact, I never heard the word "church" in any of my relationships. I dated one guy right out of college, and we were engaged for two years. He took me to his church by default, meaning I told him we need to start going to church, and he went along with it.

Isaiah was different. He was a man that wanted Christ, and all of Christ. Christ was first in his life and a priority. I was coming out of the world and settling down from making so many bad decisions in life.

When I met Isaiah, I was also battling endometriosis and a brain pituitary tumor that I shared with you earlier. Isaiah had a gift of healing. He put his hands on my problem and prayed over it, and I was healed by faith.

I knew in my heart that he was the one. God had confirmed it, and I was blessed to have him in my life. He taught me about the Sabbath. I had never heard of the Sabbath.

He also informed me that we were going to be married once I become baptized as an Adventist Christian. I was definitely okay with that.

We were married five months later. After he told me that, we both knew what we wanted. We were done with making dumb choices and making tons of mistakes in life. We knew we both loved Jesus, and we knew we wanted to raise a family. So, we didn't waste any time.

God had made it crystal clear that He was my husband. And I have not once regretted it. Not only did he become my husband, but he became my best friend.

I didn't grow up with a strong family bond; I just existed. I was like the Cinderella girl, who everyone looked over, and rejected. I grew up so hardcore. I had to learn how to be soft and patient; I believe that's why God blessed me with all girls and no boys.

I was also the one who had to prove themselves so that I could be considered or liked. Life was callous for me. I thank God I found Isaiah, who helped me change my life completely for the best. I genuinely believe God doesn't make any mistakes, and He proves to me over and over that He is in control and the head over my life.

A year into our marriage, I was so hard-headed, stubborn, rebellious, and did not know how to Love. I never saw love in my home. Being raised by grandparents, I saw them sleep in separate rooms, not coming together with financial decisions, my grandfather paid all the bills; my grandmother shopped, cooked, washed, and kept the house in order. They never really communicated at all, unless it was Sunday after church, gossiping about all the people at the church. But on any given day, I never saw them talk at all. They argued a lot, and that was about petty things.

So, finally, being married to the man of my dreams was a struggle. I assumed it was going to be easy, and all my worries, doubts, and fears were going to be gone.

I was so mean, and I did not trust him. I didn't even trust that he could provide for me, and I definitely didn't know or understand how to allow him to be the man of our home. I was like, what is that, and how do I do that. I was a mess, so confused, and didn't have any counsel from real women of God.

I only talked to friends for advice, and that only got me nowhere. Whereas, I should have been taking my problems and concerns to my heavenly father in prayer.

When you are married, you are one. Yes, I had to learn the hard way. Scripture says in Ephesians 5:23, "For the husband is the head of the wife even as Christ is the head of the church, his body, and is himself its Savior."

1 Timothy 2:11-15, says, "Let a woman learn quietly with all submissiveness. I do not permit a woman to teach or to exercise authority over a man; rather, she is to remain quiet. For Adam was formed first, then Eve; and Adam was not deceived, but the woman was deceived and became a transgressor. Yet she will be saved through childbearing-if they continue in faith and love and holiness, with self-control."

Through my faith and trust in the Lord, my God has shown me how to love my husband and allow him to be the head of my house and our family. This is a true blessing. God had to show me through trials that it wasn't going to be any other way but to follow what the word of God.

We as a people will never arrive at the status we think we need to be until we understand our positions as a husband or wife when we profess to be a child of God. If you are not following the ways and the covenant of God, you are under a curse and a direct attack of the enemy. And sad to say you will always have holes in your pockets, financially.

I got tired of that. I was always in lack, with the mindset I had and was never arriving at all that God intended for me to be.

It's about him, not us, His purpose, and plan of why we exist. We must follow Christ and the commands of the Almighty God if we truly want to be free in all aspects of life, spiritually, financially, health, mind, body, and soul.

Husbands are unique and special, just like we are as women. We are all wired differently, and it was for a reason. My advice to you, if you are married, please follow the commands of the Lord. Allow your husband to be what God created him to be. Stop being the man of your house, or trying to wear the pants, because it was not ordained that way. It took 13 years for me to figure it out, Hurricane Harvey making me lose all my material things and completely starting over to get my house in order.

Don't allow a hurricane to come, or a life-threatening situation to occur for you to figure out what your role is in your home. Allow God to work your problems out. Learn scripture, take the time to seek the Lord, and pray over your husband daily, make it be a part of your daily regimen.

We tend to take on too many things that don't matter when our family is our 1st priority and our most precious gift. The bible and scripture say in Mathew 6:33, "Seek ye first the kingdom of heaven and its righteousness and all these things will be added unto you."

We must trust in him people so that we can receive the promised land. Who wants to miss out on that reward? I know I do not, or I will be a fool. We come too far by faith, and there should be no turning back. Walk forward, walk in your purpose, your destiny, don't worry about your past and past mistakes, start now. Today is the first day of the rest of your life. My favorite quote is, "I can do all things through Christ that strengthens me," Proverbs 4:13.

I wasted so many years being stubborn. Do you know what the word of God says about stubbornness? There are several scriptures about stubbornness. The one that was most prominent to me was, "They are darkened in their understanding, being alienated from the life of God because of the ignorance that is in them due to the hardness of their hearts." Ephesians 4:18.

I was ignorant, foolish, not seeking the word of God wholeheartedly. I wasn't taught or raised to submit to my husband. I got my "do it my way" attitude from my grandmother. That was definitely not the way of thinking.

The way to a healthy marriage is to follow God's plan, his blueprint, the word of God. His approach will give you freedom, confidence, and blessings. Money was my God for many years. I wanted to do things my way and spend money the way I wanted to spend it, and not consult with my husband about it. I didn't want him to tell me I couldn't do things I wanted to do.

Those days are over. I no longer want to do things my way. You win when you do things God's way. He says in Psalms 84:11, "No good thing will I withhold from those who walk uprightly." Greater is he that is in me, than he that is in the world," 1 John 4:4. These two verses are used to encourage Christians that they can overcome any perceived obstacle in their life. Life should be easy for us, but we make it hard by the way we think.

My husband would have to tell me all the time that my peace comes from God. When you do things your way, you will not arrive at all that God has for you. Trust me, I was stubborn and hard-headed. It was in my genes, and it was how my upbringing conditioned me to think. A quote that my grandparents would quote is, "a hard head would make a soft behind." Meaning, you are not going to get anywhere being hard-headed.

How Successful People Win:

- The most important person you ever talk to is yourself, so be careful what you say
- The most important person you will evaluate is yourself, so be careful what you think
- The most important person you will love is yourself, so be careful what you do

Success is:

- Knowing your purpose in life
- Growing to reach your maximum potential
- Sowing seeds that benefit others

Keep in mind that whoever loves money never has enough of it; whoever loves wealth is never satisfied with his income.

Grow to your potential, concentrate on continual improvement, forget the past, focus on the future, and help others. Be strong and courageous, don't give up on God, because He won't give up on you.

Prepare for your overflow and Harvest. He wants to bless you. There's one thing I want to leave with you, and that is, "Seek ye first the Kingdom of righteousness, and all these things shall be added unto you," Mathew 6:33.

You can't go wrong when you put God first. I'm a testimony of that, my friend. All things are possible with King Jesus. He is the way, the truth, and the Light. And there is no other like him. He is a man that shall not lie. The devil is the liar, and he comes to steal, kill, and destroy your peace, and your lives.

Don't allow him to win folks; your salvation is on the line. And you must choose, eternal peace, or hell, the lake of fire.

So, what will you choose today? O ye of little faith, maturity, and wisdom comes from the Lord. Seek him today wholeheartedly. It's not by accident that you chose to read this book about a woman who chose Jesus and did not allow anyone or anything to turn her the other way. Not drugs, not alcohol, and not sin, because we all fall short of his glory, but who chooses to be free, is free indeed.

CHAPTER 8

LOSING A FRIEND

I lost a very dear friend, Tamera Rivera, on Wednesday, September 12, 2018. It was heartbreaking. The hardest I had to experience since the passing of my great grandfather that raised me, whom I spoke so highly of in my book.

She died giving birth to her daughter. I never thought losing a friend would be so hard. It was hard for me because she was so anointed and so passionate about the Lord.

She wanted to make sure she honored him in all that she did. She didn't party at clubs, drink, smoke, use profanity. She had a smile that would light up 50 states.

She was a loving wife, mother of 2 adorable sons, ages 2 and 4. Just the thought of them growing up without a mother is hard. Tamera was a stay at home mom who passionate about teaching her sons about Jesus.

She was a homemaker and loved it. I mean, how many people enjoy the duties of being a stay at home mom? Right.

GLORIA PATTERSON

Tamera was born on January 5, 1992, in Los Angles, California. Through the Love of Christ, she gave up working as a CNA to become a full-time stay at home mother. Her children were her pride and joy.

She loved photography, drawing, music, dancing, singing, and spending quality time with her family. She was an amazing counselor, chef, teacher, wife, mother, sister, friend, and a Powerful Woman of God. My biggest inspiration as a friend, because she was so young and so passionate about perfecting her character for Christ and helping the homeless. Tamera would give you her last. That's the kind of heart she had. A big heart for souls, a prayer warrior, and happy the majority of the time I knew her.

We became good friends after knowing each other for only two years, but it felt like we had been knowing each other for years because it was nothing fake about her. She made you feel like a true friend, comfortable to talk to, and never gossip about anyone.

Her love was limitless, and her sacrifice for her children was matchless. I could stay on the phone with her for hours because we both would have so much to say. We had a lot in common with having to Godly husbands that preach the gospel of Jesus Christ. We never had a dull moment.

God reminded me through the pain that he gives his toughest battles to his soldiers, and we are only visitors in this place. My prayers will forever be for her husband and two boys. How amazing their mother was! She was the greatest of all times! Bless her soul.

Quote for Tamara Rivera

"Until We Meet Again"

Those special memories of you will always bring a smile if only I could have you back for just a little while. Then we could sit and talk again just like we used to do. You always meant so very much and always will do too. The fact that you are no longer here will always cause me pain, but you're forever in my heart until we meet again. She has left behind 2 beautiful boys, and a Spirit-Filled husband, Phillip Rivera who continues to carry on her legacy.

When my friend passed away, I began to realize even more how short life is. I had to reevaluate what I was not doing with my time, and if I was using my time wisely. I had to do a checklist of things like, My relationship with God, reading and studying my word, Family time, how much quality time was I spending with my family, how much time was I spending with my husband, personal time for myself, my health, eating habits, exercise time, was I doing something at least 30 minutes a day to help my body.

Have you assessed your life lately? Are you allowing your time to getaway? Are you managing your emotions, and holding yourself accountable for your actions and activities?

Its time to sit down and look at your life, your sphere of influence, and evaluate how much time you are spending in God's word.

If you have a family, how much time are you spending with them to help them grow spiritually because just going to church is not enough. You need morning and night devotion. In the mornings, if you only have time to pray with them because of your full-time job, then make sure you are praying with your family, children, and spending enough time with them at night. Life is too short to focus on things that are not remotely important.

I had decided to start a new business called It Works. Because I realized that we needed residual income, and our two incomes were not enough money. Yes, I had my Mary Kay business as well, but I didn't see results fast enough. I felt like I needed to add something easier to my plate.

Its like trial and error, we know we must do something different when you are not receiving the results you are looking for, but we also have to fail at something for it to register maybe I'm not in a season to prosper in this right now.

All I know is if you keep doing what you been doing, you are going to keep getting what you have been getting. And sad to say, I was not making any money in Mary Kay. It is an amazing business and company, but I wasn't prospering in it.

I had met several people in the years I was in Mary Kay and went through a lot of people I recruited that didn't stick with me, and here and there customers.

When we moved to Ohio, I felt that it was time for me to give up everything old that I had been doing and not prospering in. I had been so tired of being tired. Struggling financially, working a dead-end job, meaning I definitely wasn't going to make a whole lot of money.

You can only make so much as a paraprofessional. I liked working in school because I had the flexibility I needed for my family. I had my summers off, and my evenings with my children, but as time went on, I was like I can't keep doing this type of work, I wasn't making any money.

With three girls as daughters, not only could they eat us out of a home, but they needed things, clothes, shoes, school activities. We had lots of bills and debt that had accumulated over the years between me and my husband.

I was like enough is enough and began to go to war with God about our financial situation. Then Hurricane Harvey came, and we flooded out and had to move, and started our entire life over in Ohio. All I got to say is, "God, do it!" He may not come when we want him, but he is always on time. I live by that principle. I never thought Ohio, but I knew that change was coming.

I've learned through my living never to question God. Why? We are just to move forward and continue to pray because God will always make a way. I'm grateful for all my learning experiences and everything I've encountered in Texas.

Conquer Your Fears and Win

Texas was a great state, and Katy, TX alone was a great city and place to raise a family. I birth all my children in Houston, TX. And I'm grateful for the blessings, but little did I know was that was not going to be my final destination. That was just a starting point in our life.

Living in Columbus, OH, has become a place of opportunity, growth, and a new turning point of living. I am so excited about the experience here. I have felt so liberated being here. Like embarking into a fresh start of life and living. My husband landed a profound career opportunity and work, and I also did, and the girls are at a #1 school. Life has been great, and I know that the Best is yet to come, and I must trust the process of what God is doing.

When my friend, Tamera died, I had to realize how short life was. I mean, we know it is, but when someone close to you dies at a young age, it's like a light bulb going off in your brain like a reminder that life can be short. I need to be happy, appreciate the journey, embrace it, and live to my fullest potential. Let Go and Let God! Stop sweating the small stuff. Realize where you are in life, pray to God to continue to order your steps, and allow him to be your guide.

I'm embracing my journey, and you should too! Get some order in your life, unclutter your brain, and detox. Life is what you speak of it to become. We live in our conversation, what you talk about you'll be about, what you think about you bring about. Watch and pay attention to what you are speaking and inviting into your life. When you awake every morning, it's by God's grace. You are alive, so be grateful and thankful. God has so much in store for us. We must allow him to lead the way. Embrace your journey, and be glad that God has kept you thus far.

What I would like for you to do right now is, sit down in a quiet place, take out a sheet of paper, and truly assess your day, week, and month. Example as follows: You will write your time beginning at

6am: <u>awake, pray, and devotion</u>_____

GLORIA PATTERSON

7am:
Breakfast_____

8am: Off to work_____

9am_____

10am_____

11am_____

12am_____

1am_____

12noon_____

1pm_____

2pm_____

3pm_____

4pm_____

5pm: Your workday is completed!

Now access the rest of your day, what are you doing with the rest of your time? When you look at the rest of the hours that you have, it will show you if you are on track with spending time with God, your purpose in Life, or any family things you are doing to grow your family. Also, document time that you need to regroup, exercise, plan your meals or hobbies. Its always good to replenish yourself and the needs of your body. It will also remind you and show you that God gives us the time we need. We just have to use our time wisely. Hold ourselves accountable. God is good all the time, all the time, God is good.

6PM_____

7pm_____

8pm_____

9pm_____

10pm: <u>this is the time you should stop everything you are doing and get the adequate amount of rest that you need.</u>

Our body needs rest. Without the proper amount of rest, our body loses nutrition and enzymes. Purposely plan your day and your life. It takes 21 days to detox our brain and thinking. All you must do is consistently do the same thing for 21 days, and that will develop a habit.

I pray you have enjoyed my book and the encouraging quotes and the new journey needed for you to become a better improved new you, mind, body, and soul. Life is about what you make it to be, so Live it wisely and enjoy every moment God gives you the breath of life. It's a blessing to be alive each day you awake, because we are not promised tomorrow, don't forget. Improve your quality of life by taking everything in God in prayer and the necessary steps to improve your quality of life. God wants to help develop your character more and more each day. Surrender your will to Him and let go and Let God. Do not stay in a mindset of old thinking, renew your mind through prayer and God's word, the bible. Be blessed and stay encouraged! God is not finished with you yet. Write your story and claim the promises of God over your life.

ABOUT THE AUTHOR

I am a devoted wife to Isaiah Hezekiah Patterson. I married my husband on September 22, 2004. We have three daughters together, Elisabeth, Hannah, and Naomi. I also have a stepdaughter, Sarah Patterson.

I enjoy inspiring women to believe in themselves, exercise their faith, and overcome adversity, by shifting their mindset. I am a firm believer in whatever the mind can perceive it can achieve. Reading motivational books inspires me to lead and mentor others to success. Stay afloat by quoting the promises of God.

Believing is a state of mind, whatever you put your mind too, just do it, don't allow no one or anything to stop you or get in the way! You are a child of a king, and you were designed and created to become your best you. My favorite scripture and promise in God's word are, "You can do all things through Christ that strengthens you!" Don't stop or quit until you WIN!

My book was written to inspire any woman or man who has been told that they are not good enough. We are all good enough. We are fearfully and wonderfully made, according to Psalms 138:14.

Your power is in your Thinking! So, let go of your insecurities, doubts, and fears, and "Conquer Your Fears and Win."

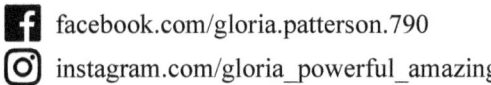

facebook.com/gloria.patterson.790

instagram.com/gloria_powerful_amazing

www.ingramcontent.com/pod-product-compliance
Lightning Source LLC
Chambersburg PA
CBHW052122110526
44592CB00013B/1713